The historic core of York. In this vertical air-photograph, the Minster (upper centre) can be clearly seen, set across the centre of the Roman Legionary Fortress. The fortress was placed between the River Ouse (which cuts across the lower left corner of the photograph) and the River Foss, which meanders down the right side to join the Ouse near York Castle (bottom centre). Photo: Meridian Airmaps Ltd.

Introduction

For most of the past 2000 years York has been an important place by the standards of each passing era. Geography and geology are at the root of this continuity, for York is at the centre of a natural communications network. It lies on an easy east-west crossing of the low-lying Vale of York; the River Ouse is tidal up to this point and provides a link with the North Sea and beyond. The ease with which both troops and bulk produce could be shipped to and from the city was a key to its importance in several periods. York is sited at the place where the river cuts through the moraine land route, and where the tributary River Foss also joins the Ouse.

In this booklet we shall chart the development of York through each successive period, from its Roman foundation through the Anglian Dark Age to its Viking heyday and beyond, to the Norman takeover, the medieval apogee and the changes in recent centuries.

The first four of these periods—Roman, Anglian, Viking and Norman—take their names from groups of people who in turn dominated York. Each left a legacy of buildings, roads, property boundaries and defences which together determined the layout of medieval and thus modern York. Remember that what we think of as Roman York was not built in a day. As in any modern city, re-building was always going on, and a citizen of AD 100 would probably have been as surprised at the state of the town in AD 300 as we are. This is true for all the periods. So little is known about most of them that the only way to present a picture of each is through all the archaeological evidence available for it. Only for the later medieval period, when documents of many kinds augment the story, is a more detailed survey possible, though space will not permit it here.

Our ignorance of so much of York's buried remains is perhaps surprising in view of the city's known historical importance, but this is typical of all towns and villages. The potential rewards of archaeological study in towns have only relatively recently been appreciated, and the need for urgency understood. York's archaeology is, however, tremendously rich, with exceptionally thick occupation deposits reaching a depth in places of up to 10 m. Moreover, many of these deposits are waterlogged, which means the survival of organic materials such as wood, leather and textiles, as well as biological remains such as pollen, seeds and insects. The archaeologist can thus present a much more complete picture of ancient York than of most other British towns. Living and working conditions can in fact be brought to life in remarkable detail.

From about 1750, York was a backwater compared with places like Leeds or Sheffield, and so its buried remains of earlier ages were untouched by large-scale industrial development. In the 1950s and 1960s, large redevelopment projects did start to eat away at the underground historical archive, and at an alarming rate which could not be countered by the usual limited, summer-only, excavation campaigns. The answer could only be the establishment of a team of professional archaeologists, and in 1972 the York Archaeological Trust came into existence. Now, with a staff of over 30 specialists, it is one of the leading urban archaeological units in Britain. It has excavated approximately 25 major sites since 1972, as well as doing smaller excavations and constantly watching building-sites. Much of the story told here has come to light in this work.

York Today

The modern city has expanded well beyond its medieval nucleus, but before this time occupation was concentrated in the 106.4 hectares enclosed by the walls. Both north and south of the River Ouse, the medieval defences were more or less on the line of the Roman fortress walls and of the Roman civilian town. Within the walls, most of the buried evidence for York's history is to be found, and surviving medieval and earlier buildings can be seen.

However, apart from these obvious relics of the past, the very streets and individual properties often have an ancestry which can be traced back for a thousand years or more, for the lines of roads and boundaries have often remained unchanged. Within the area of the Roman fortress, for example, the lines of its main streets, the *via praetoria* and the *via principalis*, are echoed by Stonegate and Petergate. Across the Ouse, the sweeping curve of Micklegate reflects the need to abandon the regular Roman street grid when a new bridge was established at the site of Ouse Bridge some time in the Anglian or Anglo-Scandinavian period, after the Roman bridge 200 m. upstream had decayed. Thus York's street plan is an historical document charting the city's development, altered by succeeding generations. With constant occupation, building débris and other rubbish accumulates, so that the contours of the city's surface have changed considerably: York is now much flatter and more regular than it was before man moved in. Over the years, hollows have been filled and slopes levelled up, masking the uneven nature of the original terrain. It takes a considerable effort to imagine the site as it was when the Roman legion first camped here.

Roman York—Eboracum

All that we know of the area before the legion arrived is of small Iron Age farmsteads, seen all around the city on air-photographs, but never yet found below York itself. The Roman army's first certain occupation of York, which they called *Eboracum*, was during the period AD 71–74, when the 6000 men of *Legio IX Hispana* advanced from their previous base at Lincoln against the native tribe, the Brigantes. Roman military surveyors were renowned for their skill in choosing camp sites, and they must have picked on the easy communications as well as the good defensive position offered by the neck of land between the Rivers Ouse and Foss. The legion's buildings were of timber, and although very few have been found by excavation, they followed the standard pattern of barracks, officers' quarters, headquarters building, hospital and stores. They were protected by an earth rampart capped by a wooden palisade, and with a ditch beyond. Timber watch towers resting on four or six massive posts provided vantage-points at least along the Ouse frontage.

The clearest glimpse of the fortress in the early years has come from excavations by the York Archaeological Trust at 9 Blake Street in 1975. Several successive phases of buildings were uncovered, showing that even during the first fifty or so years building had to be renewed periodically, perhaps because of natural deterioration, but probably because it became clear that York was a valuable operational base in the long term.

The many needs of the garrison prompted both private enterprise and official development in the vicinity of the fortress. Taverns, shops and temples formed the unofficial part of this area, which was called the *canabae*. Wharves were probably built, where essential supplies brought by ship from southern England and the continent could be unloaded, and warehouses were erected between the River Ouse and the fortress. One, a grain store, was found below 39 Coney Street in 1974. It was eventually demolished because it was infested with grain beetles; the site was

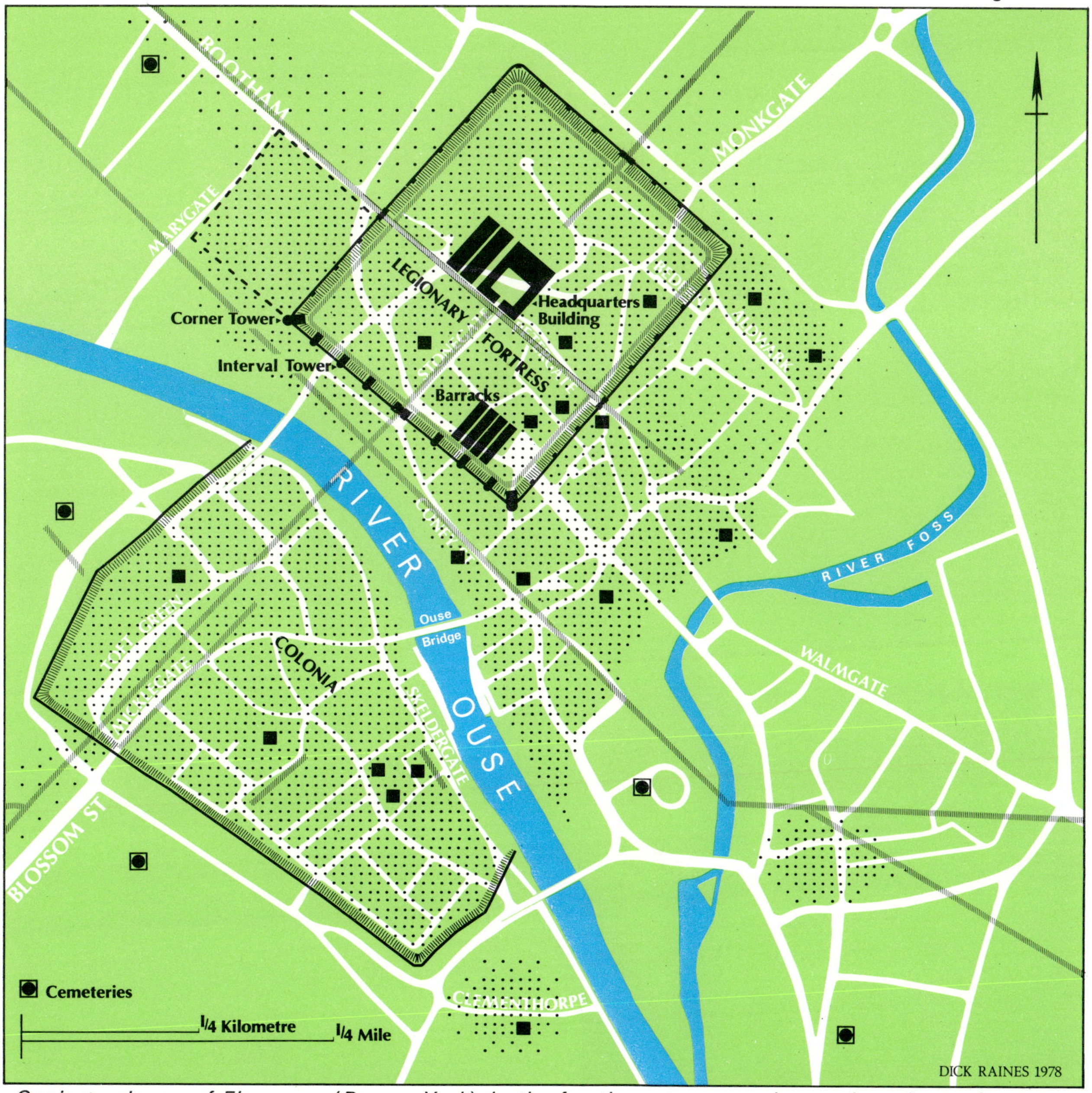

Conjectural map of Eboracum (Roman York) in the fourth century, superimposed on the modern street plan. Only the main archaeological features are indicated. Stippling: known area of occupation. Solid black squares: main archaeological sites.

sealed with a thick dump of clay, and a new store built at a higher level.

York's continuing prosperity was assured when the imperial authorities decided to re-build the fortress in stone. An inscription found in King's Square in 1854 records that work on the east gate was in hand in AD 107-108, and it is likely that the transformation was completed within a short time. The fortress remained the headquarters of Northern Military Command until the final withdrawal of Roman troops about AD 400. The Ninth Legion, however, did not remain throughout. Shortly after AD 108, it was withdrawn from Britain and replaced at York by *Legio VI Victrix*, transferred from Germany and brought to York after a spell working on and near Hadrian's Wall. The Emperor Hadrian himself must have visited Eboracum during his British visit in AD 122.

While the Roman army remained, parts at least of the walled circuit were several times refurbished. Their most spectacular strengthening came soon after AD 300, when the south-western front of the fortress, that facing the River Ouse, had multangular corner towers and six hexagonally fronted interval towers added to it. They were to provide launching platforms for *ballistae* or other types of projectile throwers. Consequently, massive foundations were essential, as were seen in 1975 when one tower was totally excavated for the first time.

Remarkably few of the fortress's internal buildings have been excavated. Two still visible are fragments of a bath building below the *Roman Bath* public house in St. Sampson's Square and parts of the *principia* (headquarters building) under the Minster's crossing tower. Tiny portions of barrack blocks were recorded during the construction of the Davygate Centre in 1956, but only two substantial discoveries have since been made. The first came to light by chance during building works on the corner of Church Street and Swinegate in 1972. A subterranean passage was found which, during an all too brief excavation by the Trust, was recognized as part of a Roman sewerage system. A section of the passage 52 m. in

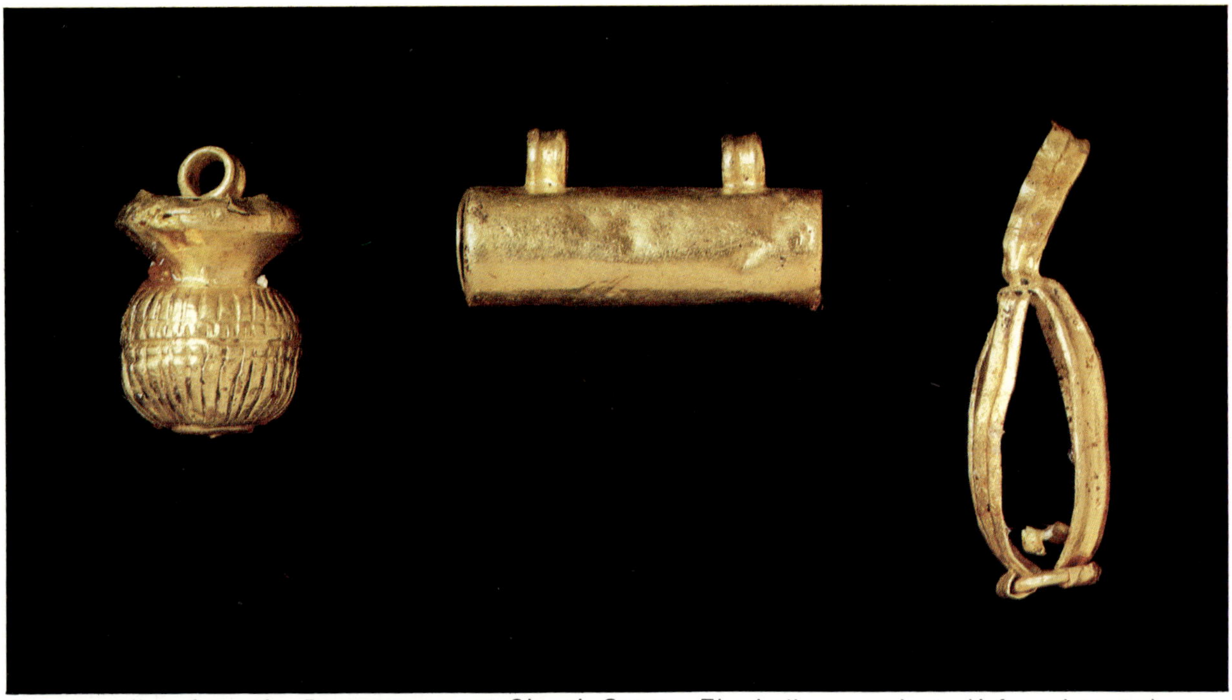

Gold jewellery from the Roman sewer at Church Street. The hollow pendants (left and centre) were probably amulets containing charms. *Photo: Mike S. Duffy*

Roman belt-plaque decorated with millefiore glass set in red, white and blue enamel. Possibly part of an officer's accoutrements.

Photo: Mike S. Duffy

length was cleared, averaging 1 m. in height and 0.45 m. in width, with its attendant Roman manhole, sluice system and subsidiary inlets. Silting had virtually blocked the system in the late fourth or early fifth century. Biological remains extracted showed that there had been much fresh water running through the passages, suggesting that the sewer carried away water from the baths revealed above. Among the many small objects which had found their way into it were several dice and gaming counters; the baths served as social clubs. A number of engraved gemstones echo the tastes of the military personnel who used the baths, while small pieces of gold jewellery show that women also frequented the place. The second major discovery was at Blake Street, where a range of rooms is thought to have belonged to an officer's house.

The Dean's Park, occupying about a quarter of the area of the fortress, keeps that part of it relatively safe from destruction. It may one day provide the opportunity for long-term research excavations, but elsewhere in the fortress no chance should be lost to trace its structure and development.

The same is true of the civilian town across the Ouse from the fortress. It was given the title of *colonia* in the early third century, a designation and distinction given to only three other British towns, Colchester, Lincoln and Gloucester. When the province of *Britannia* was divided into two parts by Severus (AD 193-211), York became capital of the northern province, *Britannia Inferior*. The few Emperors including Severus, Caracalla and Constantius who ventured to this Imperial outpost may have taken over the provincial governor's quarters which were presumably in this area. Two of them (Severus and Constantius) died here, and Constantine, who granted Christianity official recognition throughout the Empire, was in York when he was proclaimed Emperor in AD 306. At the heart of the civilian population, however, were probably prosperous merchants and local dignitaries, some of whom are known through surviving inscrip-

Roman bronze seal-box lid decorated with an eagle. *Photo: Mike S. Duffy*

Interior of the Roman sewer at Church Street, showing one of the vaulted sections. *Photo: Arthur MacGregor*

tions; and there was every kind of specialist from oculist to schoolmaster.

The origins of the *colonia* have not been explored archaeologically. The best known group of finds from it is probably the collection of mosaic pavements, some quite elaborate, dug up during the eighteenth and nineteenth centuries when there was no-one to record properly the structures to which they belonged. Substantial parts of one group of buildings have been excavated in the Bishophill area, but vast tracts of it remain unexplored. The prosperous merchants and local dignitaries who formed the backbone remain an almost unknown quantity in archaeological terms. One important new discovery is a large town house found in 1976/7 at Clementhorpe beyond the *colonia*'s probable eastern boundary. A mosaic pavement had been found here in the nineteenth century, and the recent excavation revealed a large *triclinium* (dining room) built on a terrace overlooking the river. The full extent of this impressive residence remains unknown, but it underlines the prosperity of York in the fourth century.

In the Roman world the dead were always buried outside a city's walls. At York, there were extensive cemeteries flanking the approach roads to both fortress and *colonia*. Wealthier members of both military and civilian communities were commemorated by tombstones which sometimes had portraits of the deceased, and which also provide fascinating biographical details. A good selection can be seen in the Yorkshire Museum, but as with the mosaic pavements, most have no firm archaeological association; the skeletons and the burial objects which were to accompany the dead person to the next world have been lost to us. One such group does serve, however, to introduce the nascent Christian community of Roman York, which is known to have sent its bishop to the Church council held at Arles in AD 314, for it included a Latin inscription carved in bone: *soror ave vivas in deo*, meaning, Hail, sister; may you live in God. The young woman whose skeleton lay in the enclosing coffin may have been a convert. No trace has been found of

Artist's impression of Lucius Duccius Rufinus, Standard Bearer of the Ninth Legion, based on his tombstone (first century). *Drawing: Tony Barton*

any Roman church in the *colonia*, and perhaps none will ever be found, as early Christian communities are thought to have met in private houses. Burials from another cemetery in Castle Yard seem to show some breakdown in the social order of York in the fourth century. Inscribed sarcophagi, meant to stand above ground level, were found to have been buried at a later date when they were used again to house corpses clearly not those to whom their inscriptions refer. Originally this cemetery had been used by the centurions of the garrison and their families. The desecration of its monuments while the Roman army was still there may reflect the changing composition of the army, which recruited increasingly tribesmen from the limits of Empire and beyond, who were at best semi-Romanised.

Excavation has thrown no light on the garrison of late Roman York, except for one object, the broken end of a bone comb found at Blake Street, which may have come to York in the possession of a newly enlisted recruit from Friesland. Ironically, during the fourth century, and increasingly after the Roman military withdrawal about AD 400, it was immigrants from Friesland and nearby areas of Germany and Denmark who first came to raid and then to settle in Britain, and who ultimately won control of England.

A late Roman defensive tower, part of the fortress defences, excavated at the corner of Museum Street and Lendal. Earlier buildings can be seen below it. *Photo: Arthur MacGregor*

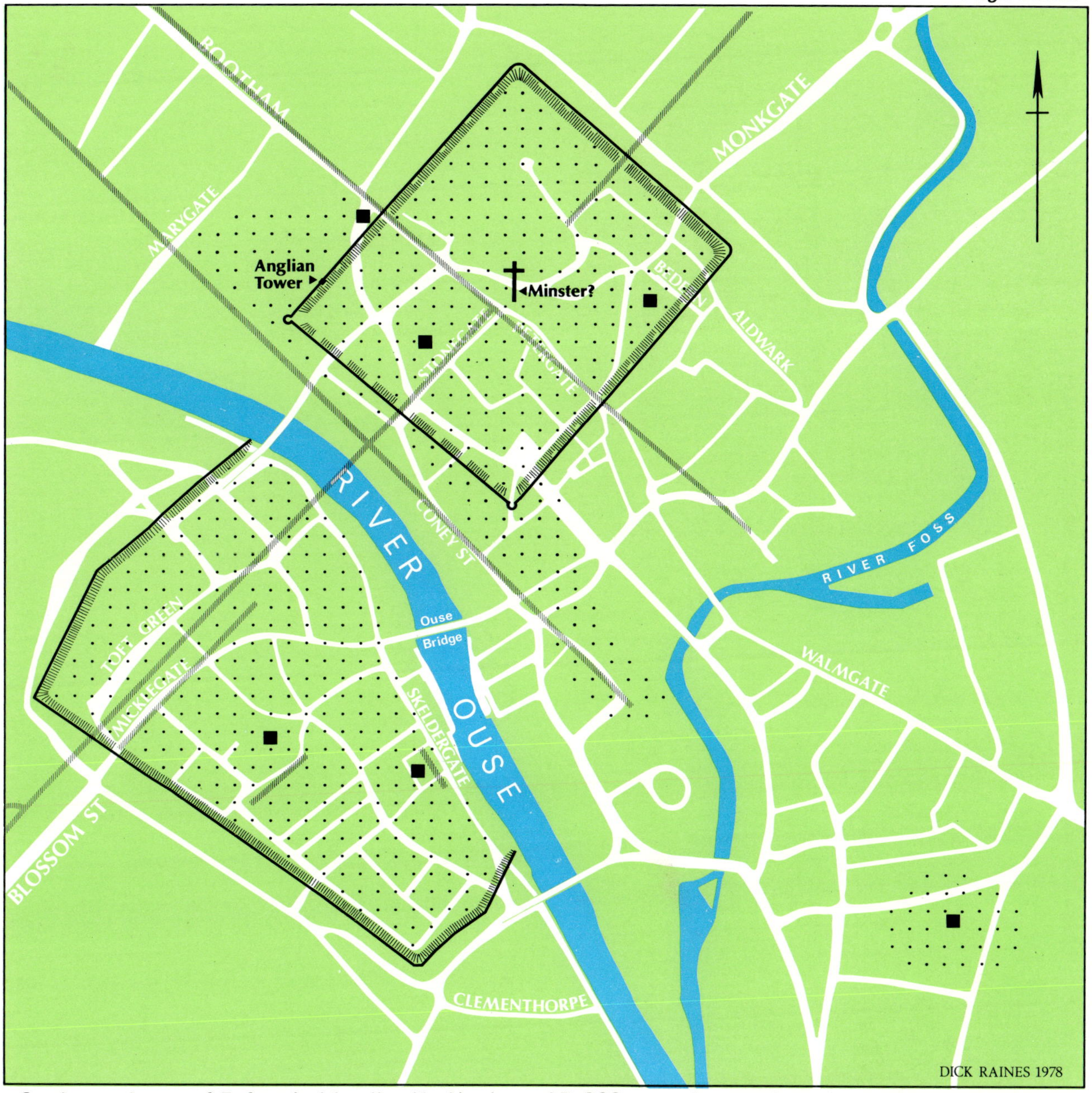

Conjectural map of Eoforwic (Anglian York) about AD 800, superimposed on the modern street plan. Stippling: presumed maximum extent of occupation. The Anglian Minster has never been found, but is thought to lie in the area indicated.

Anglian York—Eoforwic

The pagan Anglian period, from about AD 400 to AD 627, is a mystery historically and archaeologically in both York and Yorkshire. Although writers such as the monk Bede could at a rather later date refer to invasion by pagan Angles, Saxons and Jutes, coming from the area of modern North Germany, Holland and Denmark, who supposedly started to arrive in the first half of the fifth century, modern scholars disagree about when exactly this really happened. We have already seen that some Germanic peoples had been enrolled in the Roman army, and so the remains of their distinctive equipment and of their families' possessions are sometimes found in graves dating to the Romano-British period. Indeed, the commonest finds of the pagan Anglian period are cremation urns, handmade pots found in cemeteries which can include many hundred or even several thousand individual burials. There are large cemeteries at Sancton and Driffield in east Yorkshire, but the only Germanic cremation cemeteries near York, at Heworth and The Mount, are quite small. The earliest burials there may however begin at a very early date, perhaps about AD 400.

Virtually no pagan Anglian finds have so far come from the city itself, and we know little of the domestic buildings of the period. What have been seen at several sites, however, are thick deposits of soil lying on top of Roman road surfaces no longer tended by a civic or military authority. Some Roman buildings did survive in good repair throughout the entire Anglian period, including the great cross-hall of the *principia,* the

Anglian burial urn from a small cremation cemetery at Heworth, a northern suburb of York. (Yorkshire Museum.) Photo: John Bailey

central building of the fortress.

Various explanations have been put forward to account for the apparent lack of activity in York between AD 400 and AD 600. Some have claimed that large-scale flooding made low-lying parts of the city uninhabitable, but archaeologists have found no trace of such a disaster. A political reason has also been put forward; York was in a deserted border zone between areas held by the advancing Anglians and those ruled by the surviving Romano-Britons, whose kingdom, called Elmet, had its heart in the vicinity of modern Leeds. Perhaps it is simply because the population of York was so small at this time that traces of it have proved so elusive. The new invaders were not used to living in large groups, and may have had little use for the gradually decaying *Eboracum*, perhaps preferring to live in villages nearby.

Bede's writings tell in some detail of the re-introduction of Christianity to York, through the missionary work of Paulinus who converted the Anglian King Edwin, and baptised him on Easter Day, 627. The ceremony took place in a little wooden church which Edwin ordered to be built in York, or *Eoforwic* as it was by now called. Later the church, dedicated to St. Peter, was enlarged in stone and enhanced by glazed windows made by craftsmen brought over from France. It is thought to be the first of a series of churches with this name, culminating in the present Minster; but no sign of it was found in the extensive recent series of excavations there carried out by the York Minster Archaeology Office, under the direction of Mr. Derek Phillips. Nevertheless, Edwin's church probably stood quite near the present Minster.

King Edwin chose *Eoforwic* as the site for his baptism because it was the capital of his kingdom of Northumbria. Surviving Roman buildings perhaps formed a suitable nucleus for a royal palace, and the surviving fortress walls were an asset even though they had to be repaired at least twice before the arrival of the Vikings. Earth ramparts were piled up over the Roman walls, and at one point (near the corner tower) a new stone tower was constructed, of small limestone slabs, and has recently been made accessible by excavation. The precise date of the Anglian tower is not known, but it is unique in English fortifications of this era.

The trouble taken with the defences may mean that there was not just a royal entourage but also

This bone comb of late Roman or early Anglian date was found in the ruins of a Roman officer's house in Blake Street. Photo: Mike S. Duffy

Artist's impression of an Anglian huntsman, about AD 800. Details such as the horn, the shoes and the brooch fastening his cloak are based on excavated objects. Drawing: Tony Barton

a growing population in York in the seventh to early ninth centuries. One document makes it clear that Friesian traders had started to bring their goods to York, and pieces of a distinctive type of pottery, from the Rhineland, perhaps from wine-jugs, indicate the sort of luxuries they may have dealt in.

New churches show that the population was certainly growing. St. Mary Bishophill Junior still retains pieces of sculpture which show that there was worship thereabouts in the Anglian period. Bishop Wilfrid during his episcopate (664-678) renovated St. Peter's itself, the cathedral church. A surviving description of another contemporary York church, dedicated to Holy Wisdom, makes it clear that this too was a magnificent structure by the standards of the day. Unfortunately, it has not been located. However, stone and mortar did not provide the only monuments to the new religion. As well as new building techniques, traditions of classical scholarship were also brought to York by churchmen who looked to Rome for their authority, and a school grew up, staffed by clerics, which was to win international recognition.

York's most famous pupil was Alcuin, whose life (c. 732-804) spanned a period when the widespread political influence of the Northumbrian King Oswy (641-670) was only a memory, and the Midland kingdom of Mercia was dominant. Alcuin first became a master in his old school, and later was singled out by the Emperor Charlemagne to preside over the palace school at Aachen. From the continent he wrote frequently to his old friends at home, and in one of his letters the first Viking raid in Northumbria, on the monastry of Lindisfarne, is the main topic. Just over 60 years later, while rival contenders disputed the Northumbrian throne, Alcuin's beloved city (which he had described in a surviving poem) was in turn the object of Viking attack.

Anglian bronze cross brooch, of the 8th century, originally enriched with red and yellow enamel. This brooch was found with pins, coins of Eadbert of Northumbria (AD 737-58), and the remains of domestic rubbish in what must have been a small settlement outside the city near Fishergate. Photo: Mike S. Duffy

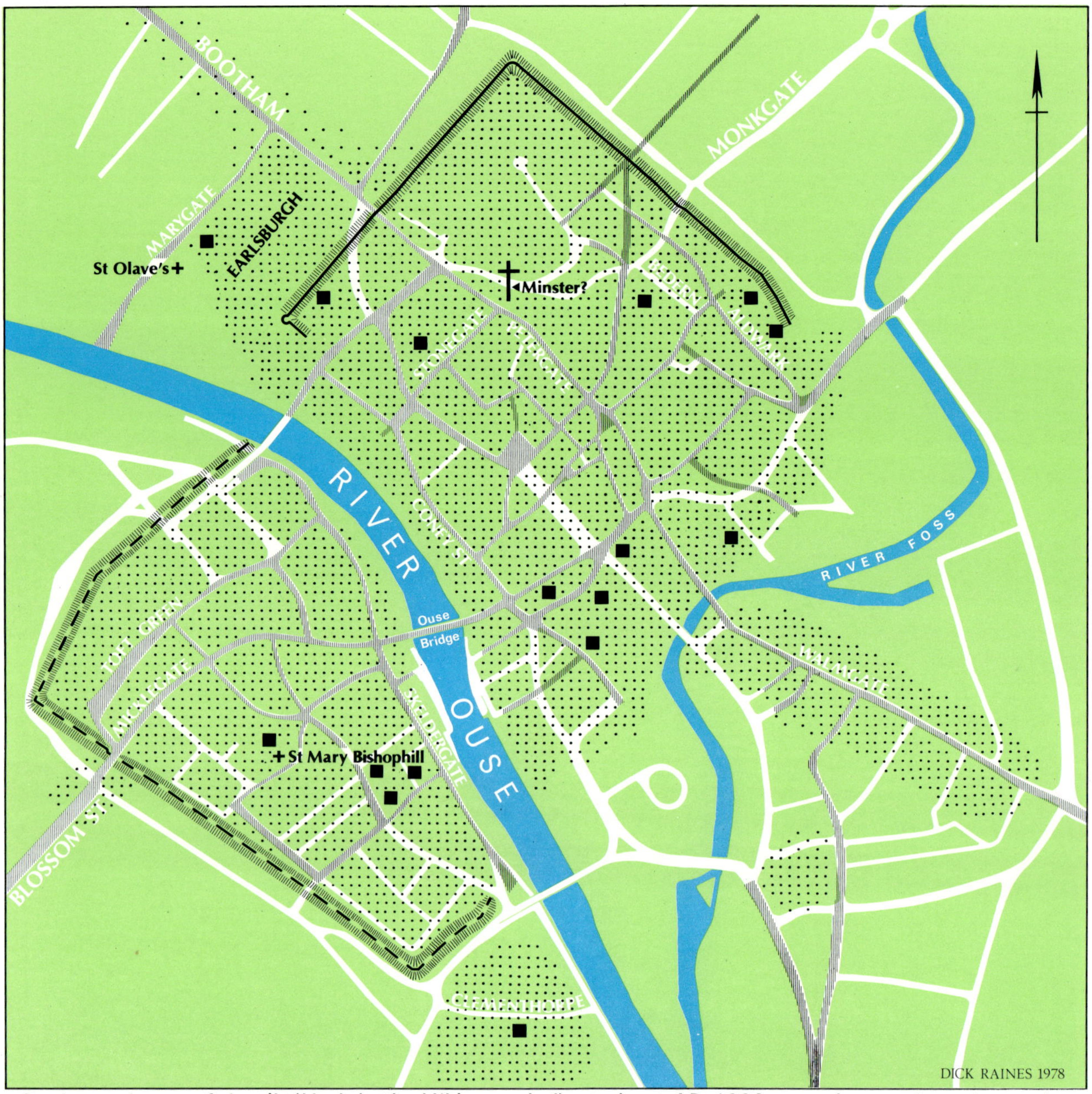

Conjectural map of Jorvik (York in the Viking period) at about AD 1000, superimposed on the modern street plan. Stippling: presumed occupation area. Solid black squares: major archaeological sites.

Viking York—Jorvik

Documents tell us that in 865 the Great Army of the Vikings seized York and defeated the Angles; in 876, part of the Great Army decided to settle permanently in and around York. For nearly 80 years, the town was to be almost continuously under direct Scandinavian rule, with a series of Danish and Norwegian kings in power; and from the early tenth century, there was a strong link with the Viking stronghold of Dublin.

Alfred's grandson, Athelstan, recaptured the town for the English in 927, but his death in 939 marked the start of a bewildering fifteen years during which six different kings, Danish, Norwegian and English, controlled York in nine separate reigns. The last Scandinavian king, the exiled Norwegian prince Erik Bloodaxe, was finally expelled in 954, and York was then ruled by a series of earls appointed by and accountable to the English kings.

Throughout all these political ups and downs, whether or not a Scandinavian king was in power, there was undoubtedly a strong Scandinavian element in York's population, perhaps reinforced by new immigrants. They seem to have been willing to adopt the material advantages of their new country. Their integration with the Anglians was probably helped immensely by their adoption of Christianity. The second Scandinavian king, Guthfrith, was buried in the Minster, and many of the rank and file settlers probably followed their king's lead.

A small group of burials excavated near St. Mary Bishophill Junior church documents an intermediate stage in the conversion, with two skeletons accompanied by grave goods in the pagan tradition buried in the Christian churchyard. A coin found with one of the bodies suggests that burial took place about 920. Evidently the Scandinavians were soon using the native coinage, and an improvement in its standard demonstrates their shrewd business sense. In the two centuries before the Norman conquest, York's mercantile prosperity increased greatly, a fact reflected in the output of the city's coin mint. This economic boom can be attributed in part to the seafaring enterprises of the new inhabitants, who voyaged far and wide bringing back exotic luxury goods such as animal furs and skins, ivory and silk for sale in York. In the export field, the city's prosperity may well have owed much to the woollen industry. The wealth and importance of *Jorvik* was attested in its size at the Norman conquest. Domesday Book records that in 1066 the city consisted of over 1600 (more probably 1800) properties, making it the second biggest city in England, eclipsed only by London.

None of these properties survives above ground today, but elements of the city's framework can still be seen. Parts of the Roman fortress wall still formed the city's defence and although the earth ramparts were themselves capped with a new clay bank in the Viking age, it is likely that the Roman multangular tower at the south-west corner was exposed to view. Across the river, the masonry of the tower of St. Mary Bishophill Junior church shows that it is of pre-Norman date, but this is the only survivor of eight churches recorded in Domesday Book, and the six others whose existence can be inferred. For all other traces of *Jorvik*, archaeology is the only source, although the forms of many streetnames in the city, particularly those which end in the element *-gate* (Old Norse, meaning *street*) suggest that much of the city's layout dates back to the Viking age.

How extensive was *Jorvik*? Within the area of the Roman fortress there have been relatively few opportunities for discovery, and in some cases where excavation has taken place, it has been found that the relevant layers had already been removed in the medieval period. Nevertheless an important Viking age cemetery with carved grave-covers and markers has been found under and near the Minster, presumably belonging to the pre-Norman cathedral's graveyard. The carvings demonstrate the artistic tastes of York's Anglo-

Débris and products of amber-working at Coppergate, including pendants, a bead and a finger-ring. Photo: Mike S. Duffy

Scandinavian society. Another discovery from within the fortress, a mould for casting a brooch, epitomises the amalgamation of English and Scandinavian tastes. The brooch was trefoil shaped, a form well-known in Scandinavia, but its decoration is a unique mixture of Scandinavian and English elements.

Across the River Ouse, scattered finds show that people were certainly living there, although if there was a defensive wall or rampart, which seems likely, it has not been traced yet in excavation. The most obvious difference between the Roman *colonia* and the present layout of the area is the sweeping curve of the main north and south

Viking age wooden cup and bowl (left), fine examples of the wood-turner's art. (Right) Modern replica made by a local wood-turner. Photo: Mike S. Duffy

Overhead view of three late 10th century wooden buildings discovered at Coppergate. Photo: Mike S. Duffy

street, Micklegate, leading to Ouse Bridge. Probably first built in the Viking age, this remained the only bridge across the Ouse until 1863, and led across to the area currently thought to be the commercial nucleus of *Jorvik*.

Here in the Coppergate-Castlegate-Ousegate-Pavement area, beyond the east wall of the Roman fortress, various Viking age objects have been found by chance over the last 250 years, and here in 1972, below Lloyd's Bank at 6-8 Pavement, the first significant excavation of Viking age deposits in York took place. There were 9 m. of buried archaeological layers. Amid the débris from timber buildings of Viking age date, thousands of leather fragments preserved in the damp soil conditions showed that the buildings had been leather-workers' premises. This was confirmed by the organic remains—seeds, pollen and insects—which were of species likely to be found in a tannery.

The most recent and large-scale examination of *Jorvik* has been in progress in Coppergate since 1976. Four adjacent tenements running back from Coppergate/Pavement to the River Foss are under excavation. Work has so far centred on subsidiary buildings, probably workshops, behind the street frontage. Surviving in places up to a height of 1.8 m., these are amongst the best-preserved Viking age buildings ever discovered, and can be dated on the basis of coins lost in their earth floors to about 960-985. For the first time, they have given an impression of what *Jorvik's* townscape was like, in this case single-storey buildings with floors up to 1 m. below ground level, resting on squared foundation beams and having walls of horizontal oak planks supported only on the interior by squared uprights. The roofs were either of thatch or of shingles. The sunken side walls were preserved by the soil outside, but the key factor was that when the buildings were left derelict (for whatever reason) their interiors were used as a rubbish dump, which quickly became waterlogged, thus also sealing the timber walls and protecting them from decay. The débris is itself interesting, as it consists of wood-workers' waste, including wood chips and

Artist's impression of a Viking merchant of the tenth century. Belt, cloak-fastening, embroidery and footwear are based on excavated evidence, as are the scales he holds for weighing precious metals. Drawing: Tony Barton

Oblique view of the central building, in the photograph opposite, showing the excellently preserved oak walls and upright supports standing to a height of 1.75 m. *Photo: Mike S. Duffy*

shavings, wooden bowls and a cup, and some of the tools used to make them. Woodworkers must have had workshops nearby, and this was independently suggested by the street name, Coppergate, an Old Norse name first recorded in 1120-35, which means 'street of the woodworkers.'

The many objects found discarded or lost in the floor levels help to build up a picture of Anglo-Scandinavian life-style. Glass beads, dress pins and brooches show the forms of popular jewellery, fragments of textile and leather represent clothes and footwear, and quantities of tools and raw materials demonstrate the range of crafts and trades that were practised. Amber in both a raw and a worked state, testifies to jewellery manufacture; antler combs and bone objects point to major antler- and bone-working industries; spindle-whorls and grindstones are the by-products of cottage industry. The animal bones will eventually tell us about both animal husbandry and diet, and oyster shells reflect an important food. Pottery fragments testify to local trade, large amounts coming from Lincolnshire.

The property boundaries and building lines throw a final interesting light on *Jorvik's* development. Laid out a thousand years ago, these lines did not change until modern times, and although redevelopment now often amalgamates several old properties, the boundaries of large new buildings frequently still reflect a Viking age origin. Glimpses of levels older than the tenth century seem to reveal buildings of a completely different type, made from withies woven around vertical stakes and planks. As the excavations proceed, more such structures are being revealed. Both their purpose and the meaning of the change have yet to be discovered.

There is still much scope for exploring *Jorvik*—for instance, near the churches of St. Denys and St. Margaret in Walmgate. Both go back before 1066, so there may have been intensive Viking age occupation in this area, which lies across the River Foss from Coppergate but is within the medieval city walls. What was here, and whether there were any pre-Norman defences, is at present entirely unknown.

Two specific sites might well tell us something about the Viking age rulers of the city. The King's palace may well have been in or near King's Square/King's Court, for the modern name is a direct reflection of the Old Norse name, *Conungsgurtha*. It may have been built around the surviving remnants of the Roman east gatehouse. This site is one of the most important in the whole Viking world, and would repay intensive excavation.

One step down the aristocratic ladder, but still of national interest, is the residence of the earls who governed *Jorvik* for the English kings. It probably lay in Museum Gardens, now covered by the ruins of St. Mary's Abbey. This at any rate is the place which Drake, an early eighteenth century historian of York, refers to as *Earlsburgh*, a name of pre-Norman form which means 'the earl's headquarters'. An additional pointer is the proximity of St. Olave's church, which is known to have been built by Earl Siward, who died in 1055. It was presumably for his own use, and is likely to have been near to his residence; but what this residence was like, only excavation may tell.

Although the Norman's takeover in 1067-69 did not wipe out either the strong Scandinavian element in the population, or the links with Scandinavia, William the Conqueror's devastation of York and Yorkshire in 1069, coupled with his castle-building enterprises, meant that Norman York of 1100 looked markedly different from Anglo-Scandinavian *Jorvik* of 1066. Over half of the houses which stood in 1066 were destroyed or derelict at the time of the compilation of Domesday Book in 1086, and when the city was re-built and began to prosper again, it was increasingly susceptible to new styles, fashions and influences brought by the new Norman overlords.

A lead alloy brooch of the tenth century, decorated with cross and tendril motifs; found in the Coppergate excavation. *Photo: Mike S. Duffy*

Norman York

For the defeated but still hostile inhabitants of York, the first years of Norman rule were dramatic and bloody. To secure his position in the north of his new kingdom, William himself apparently ordered the erection of the first castle in 1068, and garrisoned it with 500 picked knights. So intense was the local hostility to the new invaders, that following an attack on this first castle early in 1069, a second fortification was deemed necessary and was built before Easter of that year. Even so, both castles were again attacked and destroyed by a combined Anglo-Danish force within the same year. William's response was swift. The King spent Christmas at York in 1069; the castles were immediately re-built and part of the city was destroyed in the re-building. To reinforce the point, the city and countryside were ravaged with a thoroughness that has gone down in history as 'the Harrying of the North'; some areas of land remained barren for years as a result.

The two re-built castles seemed to have secured the Norman grip on the city, however, as well they might, for the easternmost was now protected by an extensive water defence, a large lake created by damming the Foss, probably somewhere near where Castle Mills Bridge stands today. This lake was to remain a major feature of York until modern times; the name of Foss Islands Road commemorates it.

Of the two castle thus re-built in 1069, one became York Castle. Its typical motte, or defensive mound, still stands with the thirteenth century Clifford's Tower on top. Its sister motte, across the river, we now know as Baile Hill. In its present condition, wooded and without any sign of timber or stone fortification, its bailey destroyed, it is typical of the fate of many of the castles erected all over England. It was already apparently disused by 1268, and by the second half of the fifteenth century had become common property and was leased for grazing. Its modest history however has made it more accessible than Clifford's Tower to archaeologists. The motte had been built up of horizontal layers of soil. Débris of the eleventh century was recovered from beneath the mound. On the summit, a large central rectangular timber structure, possibly a tower, was erected later in the Norman period. A flight of steps once faced with wood led up the side of the motte from the bailey to the top.

At Clifford's Tower, work done in 1902 to underpin the mound showed that, like Baile Hill, it was thrown up in layers. Extensive traces of burnt timber work also found below the present summit may have been the result of the burning of 1190, when the castle was sacked in an anti-Jewish riot, killing those Jews who had taken refuge there, a particularly unpleasant episode in the history of later Norman York.

Apart from the castles, it also seems that the city defences were strengthened and heightened at this time. Behind the Yorkshire Museum, at the site of the Anglian Tower, the Anglo-Scandinavian rampart (here dating to about 900) was heightened and capped by a timber breastwork. Only the stretch of defences curving out from York Castle to Walmgate Bar may have been constructed anew at this period. In addition, the principal gates of the city were probably now either built anew, or as at Bootham Bar, re-built on a Roman predecessor. The one exception is Monk Bar. The principal early medieval gate on this side of the city was still the ancient Roman *porta decumana*, some 300 m. north-west of the present bar, which is after 1300. Bootham Bar retains the earliest Norman work; its outer arch is of about 1100 or earlier. The arches of the other bars are later. By the early thirteenth century, the bars already had an upper storey above the line of the wall-walk.

Another major area of the Norman impact was in the Church. As we have already seen, a Christian church had existed at York from at least 627, and apparently by the time of the Conquest an imposing Saxon Minster stood within the immediate area of the present one, though its exact position is unclear. The chronicles tell us that the

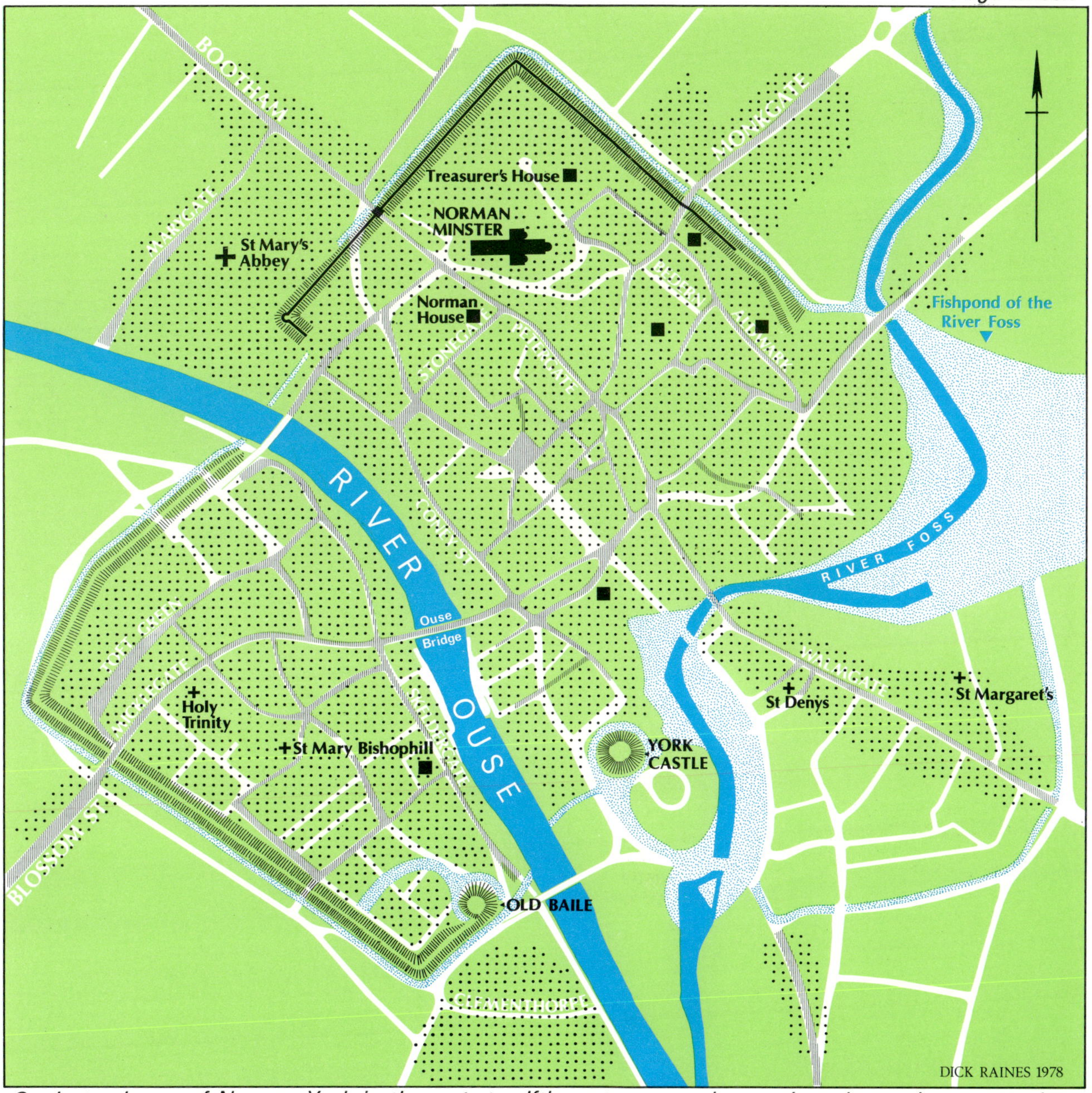

Conjectural map of Norman York in the early twelfth century, superimposed on the modern street plan. Heavy black stippling: presumed area of occupation. Fine blue stippling: water defences. Solid black squares: archaeological sites and major monuments.

tough new Norman Archbishop, Thomas of Bayeux (1070-1100) found the old church burnt, doubtless as a result of the rebellion of 1069, and re-roofed and restored it. In 1079 the Danes came again to York and destroyed the re-built church. Thomas then began to build an entirely new large church, and it was this new building that was revealed during recent excavations connected with the major restoration of the Minster. It had a wide nave without aisles, north and south transepts with apsidal chapels, and an apsidal east end. Its walls contained much re-used Roman stone, and it seems clear that such stone was relatively easily come by. Indeed, it may be that there were substantial Roman buildings visible round the Minster as late as the Norman Conquest. Inside, this re-used stone was plastered and painted with red lines to look like newly quarried and dressed ashlar blocks. This re-use of Roman stone in the new Norman Minster also has other implications. The ancient layout of the Roman legionary fortress, and particularly the area of the *principia*, was abandoned, for Archbishop Thomas' new church was built at an ungainly 45° angle across the Roman alignment. Like the building of the castles, with their scant regard for people's homes, the siting of the new Norman church cut arrogantly across established lines in favour of the correct liturgical alignment. In 1137, the Minster was again damaged by fire, and eventually re-built while Roger of Pont l'Evêque (1154-1180) was Archbishop. It now had two western towers, aisles to the nave, new transepts, a crypt and a new choir with a square east end. Some of this work may still be seen in the existing undercroft.

Elsewhere in the city, documents and architectural evidence together show how the Church flourished under the Norman stimulus. St. Mary's Abbey and the Priory of the Holy Trinity, Micklegate, were founded and new parish churches built or re-built. Good Norman work can still be seen at St. Mary Bishophill Junior, Holy Trinity Micklegate, and St. Michael's Spurriergate. Elsewhere, it is a matter of a surviving doorway, a window, or a tower.

Early thirteenth century iron shovel found near the kiln it was used to stoke: Coppergate.
Photo: Mike S. Duffy

Only one church containing work of this period, however, has been fully excavated. At St. Helen-on-the-Walls, off Aldwark, the complex development of a small parish church has been elucidated. It started as a small rectangular building, possibly of late Anglo-Scandinavian date. A small square chancel was first added, and then itself extended later. At the same time, the nave was widened and other re-building undertaken. This work probably spans the Norman period.

Any other evidence for life in Norman York is much more elusive. For instance, the remains of only two town houses, both of stone, survive

Seal of Snarrus the toll-collector: probably twelfth century. *Photo: Mike S. Duffy*

above ground. One, a complete building of about 1080, forms the core of one wing of Gray's Court, now incorporated in the Treasurer's House. The other, just off Stonegate and dated about 1180, is part of a typically Norman building, with its hall on the first floor, reached probably by an outside stair. The ground floor or undercroft was used probably as a store or for some such purpose. The rough tooling of the stone suggests that the building was originally plastered. One of its upstairs windows still survives, a good example of later Norman domestic architectural style. In High Ousegate, the remains of a timber-framed house may also be of Conquest date, for a hoard of coins of Edward the Confessor (1042-1066) was found within its construction.

Elsewhere in York, only excavation has revealed anything of other houses. At Skeldergate in the south-west part of the walled city, and at Aldwark in the north-east, slight remains of two more have been excavated, in both cases apparently of stone and substantially built. Not only was building stone easily available at this time, but the Norman Conquest, despite its inauspicious beginnings in York, must have stimulated building in the city. At Bedern, for instance, the demand for stone in the twelfth century was dramatically illustrated in the attempt, at least partially successful, to rob the legionary fortress wall where it runs parallel to St. Andrewgate, a stretch that had lost its defensive role. Here the huge millstone grit blocks of the wall's footings were found ready to be removed, with wooden levers and runners still *in situ* beneath them. Flooding groundwater, in an age before efficient pumps, probably defeated this particular attempt.

It is primarily from excavation, too, that knowledge comes of everyday life in Norman York.

Artist's impression of a Norman knight, about AD 1080, wearing a surcoat of chain-mail, a conical iron helmet with characteristic Norman nose-piece, and boots and spurs of the period. His body-length shield and broadsword were standard equipment. *Drawing: Tony Barton*

Baile Hill, all that remains of the motte of York's second castle. *Photo: Peter Addyman*

Work at Coppergate has produced a particularly good collection of finds. They include an iron shovel lying beside a tile-built hearth; and two fine wooden box-lids, one decorated with domed bronze nails and originally with marquetry inlay, the other of closely woven rushes with a plaited rush handle, also date from this period. A plank of wood with a round central hole was recognizably a seat over the latrine pit into which it had fallen. Like other wooden objects from Coppergate, it was remarkably well preserved. Similarly, at Skeldergate, many rubbish and cess pits were found behind the main house, ranging from 1 m. to 3 m. in diameter, and up to 2 m. in depth. Some showed signs of having been re-dug and re-used; one was timber-lined; a group of three had a wicker lining.

Twelfth century latrine-seat, lying in its cess-pit: Coppergate. *Photo: Mike S. Duffy*

At the bottom of one of these latter pits was a quantity of leather offcuts, suggesting leather-working nearby. This adds to the evidence of increasing industrial activity. The remains of a bead-worker's workshop were recovered during building operations in the Shambles, and it seems also that the large bronze foundry excavated near Bedern was established before 1200. On the site of W. H. Smith's new shop in Coney Street, a substantial stone wall of this period was seen, strongly suggesting improvement of the water-front, a necessary and confident prelude to York's continuing rise in the centuries to follow.

The foundations of the Norman house excavated at Aldwark: holes left by the now vanished timber pilings can be clearly seen.
Photo: Arthur MacGregor

Medieval York

York was at the height of its wealth and influence between 1200 and 1450. For most of that time it ranked second in the kingdom only to London, and indeed was for whole years together, especially during the Scottish wars of the fourteenth century, the seat of national government, with the Crown and various departments of State actually resident at York. This increasing power and influence was echoed in an equally increasing sense of municipal dignity and corporate identity, as in so many other towns at the same period. The beginnings of local government in York may go back before the Conquest, but now the city's government emerged as an hierarchical, tight-knit and powerful organisation, jealous of its rights, privileges and freedoms, which were eventually confirmed in the two important Royal Charters of 1393 and 1396, the latter of which turned the city into a county borough.

Physically, too, York was changing. From the mid-thirteenth century the city walls had begun to be re-built in stone. The Anglo-Scandinavian bank was added to after the Norman Conquest, and this higher bank was itself further reinforced by the building of the stone wall in the thirteenth and early fourteenth centuries, though it was not until 1245 that the city finally got around to re-building in stone the Walmgate defences from Fishergate to the Foss. Henry III had also begun serious work on expanding and re-building the Castle between 1245 and 1270. It is from this period that the construction of the quadrilobal keep of Clifford's Tower dates.

Within its walls, the plan of medieval York was not greatly different from the modern, though certain prominent streets like Deangate and Piccadilly did not exist, and the rivers were spanned only by the Ouse and Foss Bridges. Generally, though, there were fewer streets within the walls than today. Outside the walls there were suburbs, principally along Bootham, Monkgate, Lawrence Street, Blossom Street and at Clementhorpe. Beyond them lay the common lands of York; large areas of open land on which its citizens could graze their animals. Areas of York's pastures survive to this day, notably the Knavesmire, Hob Moor and Heworth Moor. The walled city was by the mid-fourteenth century probably well built-up. Some of the grandest medieval houses still survive, the majority being of fifteenth century date. Good examples can be seen in Goodramgate, beside All Saints', North Street, and in the Shambles. The very fine timber-framed house on Walmgate, named in honour of York's greatest pioneer conservationist, J. Bowes Morell, is a reminder of the quality and character of this street in those days. Other great medieval buildings, such as St. William's College, the Halls of the Merchant Adventurers and the Merchant Taylors, the King's Manor and the Treasurer's House, also serve to remind us what a prosperous city could build.

Surviving houses of the humbler sort are far rarer, though the row now known as Our Lady's Row in Goodramgate, dating from 1316, is more typical of, say, artisan housing. The standing buildings cannot tell the full story of the develop-

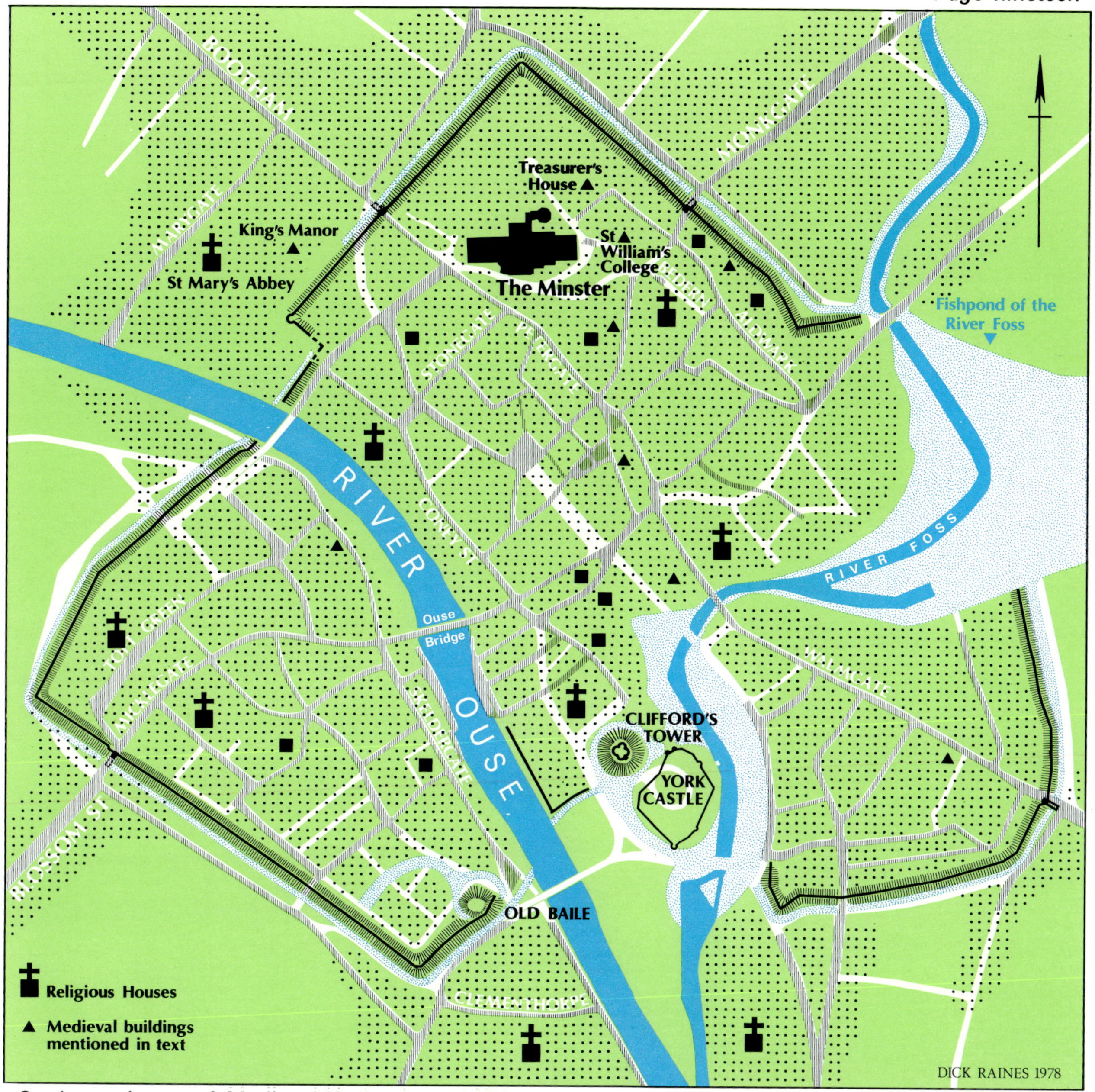

Conjectural map of Medieval York, about 1350. Heavy black stippling: presumed area of occupation. Fine blue stippling: water defences. Solid black squares: archaeological sites and major monuments.

ment of tenements and properties in medieval York. Here in particular the archaeological evidence comes into its own. Two large areas of the medieval town, at Skeldergate and Bedern, have been particularly closely investigated.

At Skeldergate, within property boundaries already ancient, timber buildings with floors of clay or boards were frequently re-built, sometimes over the filling of earlier pits. The combined effects of subsidence and levelling made the excavation and disentanglement of individual surfaces something of a problem. In the fourteenth century, there were clearly stone buildings on the site, fronting both Skeldergate and Carr's Lane, but more substantial buildings required better foundations on such a site. The best were of stone and cobbles over wooden piles. Inside one building, shallow trenches filled with broken tiles may represent supports for a timber floor, or some attempt to combat rising damp.

Similarly, the excavation of the bronze-foundry site at the Bedern showed how part of this area developed, although not primarily for domestic occupation. The foundry lay well behind Goodramgate, but its major buildings, separated in its later phases by a well-defined alleyway, were in line with existing property boundaries on the frontage. By 1200, a large hall-like timber building stood on the site, which was subsequently rebuilt in stone, perhaps with a timber-framed superstructure.

The houses of medieval York did not of course exist in a vacuum; they had to serve the people who used them, whether as homes or places of work. So in and all around every building, the evidence of human activity has been abundant: lanes, alleys, paths, wells, fences, rubbish pits, cess-pits and garderobe pits, not to mention the smaller detritus of life; the type of fortunately abundant evidence that tells us about everyday life in medieval York. Pits, usually dug to dispose of rubbish, or less commonly for storage, are to be found everywhere. Waste disposal was a major concern of every corporation in the Middle Ages. There were frequent orders in York, especially against butchers, to prevent dumping of waste

Fourteenth century gold ring from Coppergate, set with a central pearl and four amethysts.
Photo: Mike S. Duffy

into the rivers, for instance, or for the removal of dunghills. The effects may not have been all the Corporation desired, however; according to Edward II in 1322, York stank more than any other town in the kingdom. People were doubtless supposed to cart rubbish out beyond the city walls. How much more convenient to throw it into the cess-pit in the back yard or garden! And how fortunate, too, for the archaeologist today. In the earlier Middle Ages, rubbish pits were not usually lined. In the fourteenth and fifteenth centuries, however, the pits tend to become larger and deeper, often more regular in plan and more frequently and more carefully lined, on occasions with stone or brick, so that they could eventually be emptied.

From these pits comes much of the evidence of the nature of everyday life in medieval York. Pottery and animal bones form the bulk of their contents. The pottery is almost always in small pieces, though occasionally a vessel survives complete or nearly complete. Most of the pots are jugs or cooking vessels, for plates and cups were more commonly made of other materials at this period. Most of the pottery was made within the immediate locality of York, though examples from further afield and from abroad are not unknown. Animal bones are naturally plentiful, and when closely studied will probably allow us to say something about such topics as agriculture, butchery and diet. Oyster shells, equally common, form another important piece of evidence for diet in the Middle Ages.

Many thousands of individual pieces now make up the category of special finds, ranging from largely amorphous pieces of metalwork to such rare treasures as the fourteenth century gold ring set with pearl and amethyst, recently found at Coppergate.

Just as the medieval citizen was supposed to dispose of his own rubbish, so he had to organize his own water supply. So a number of wells have been found in excavations. At the Bedern foundry, a very elaborate example of thirteenth century date, lined with at least three wooden barrels, was discovered. It had been constructed within a large pit, in which a stout foundation frame of curved timbers was set, pegged and jointed together; a large timber pile was driven in at each corner, and large stones placed under the frame. On this base the barrels had been placed, one on top of the other. The barrels used were quite large, some 1.5 m. high and about 0.9 m. in diameter. They are formed of curved oak staves, each about 15 cm. wide, and unlike modern barrels, their hoops were of withies, not metal, which covered the greater part of the outside. One barrel also had a bung-hole, and what was probably the cooper's mark.

Another barrel-lined well, similar but not as well preserved, was found on the Aldwark site. It had been replaced later by yet another timber-lined well, which was far better preserved and differently constructed. Again it was set on a stout square wooden frame of curved timbers, pegged and jointed together. The upper lining in this case, however, consisted of stout planks carefully cut to size, slotted in behind four large upright corner posts, themselves securely morticed in to the base frame. This well survived to a height of 2 m., and probably dates to the later fifteenth century.

As well as evidence about rubbish disposal and water supply, archaeologists have discovered how problems of drainage were dealt with. At Aldwark, the wells were cut into the filling of a large ditch running across the site parallel to the street and the city walls.

This massive feature was excavated to a depth of 7 m. and was some 8 m. wide across the top. It was found to cut the remains of the late Anglo-Scandinavian period bank recovered from the rear of the site, and seems to have been filled up in the thirteenth century. It is probably one of the drainage ditches, several of which are mentioned in documents, usually as the 'King's Ditches'. This particular ditch is probably the historically documented and identifiable Werk-dyke, also partially excavated at the site of St.

A vertical view down the late medieval oak-lined well at Aldwark. *Photo: Arthur MacGregor*

Helen-on-the-Walls. In it was found the remains of a wooden ladder, made out of a birch pole split down its length with oak rungs slotted through carefully bored side holes. This was found against the side of the ditch, where it had lain for centuries, a mute testimonial to the problems of access confronting the diggers or clearers of the great ditch.

The foundry complex on the Bedern has been subjected to the most extensive archaeological investigations of a medieval industrial site yet carried out in York. Trade and industry, we know, must have been the essential basis of the economy of the medieval city. Up to the later thirteenth century, documents give us incidentally the names of men engaged in a wide variety of trades. Merchants and workers in the clothing industry are the commonest. The leather trade comes a close second, with metal workers, provisions traders and the building industry also represented; a fair cross-section in fact of the needs and services of a large medieval city.

From the twelfth century, the various trades were organising themselves into guilds, which by the middle of the fourteenth century were all of great importance. About 80 seem to have existed during the most prosperous period. They tried to ensure that every tradesman knew his trade, and practised it honestly in return for a fair price. The guilds were also protectionist, and tried to ensure against unfair or excessive competition. They would amount, in modern terms, to a mixture of TUC and CBI. Two guilds, the merchants and the weavers, took out Royal Charters, although most contented themselves with simply registering their guild in the city's ordinances. Other sides of their activities included social, welfare and religious work. Whatever their differences, however, they all shared in one activity, the great annual Corpus Christi procession, which by the fourteenth century included the performance of what we now know as the York Cycle of Mystery Plays, and a great deal of revelry. This was the guilds' most prominent outward manifestation of their influence and power.

Flattened lead-alloy ampulla (holy water bottle): the figure of an archbishop may represent York's celebrated St. William. *Photo: Mike S. Duffy*

Artist's impression of a Master Mason of about 1350. He wears a green jerkin over brown hose, and carries the tools of his trade, a set-square and a mason's hammer. *Drawing: Tony Barton*

Such then was the context in which the medieval craftsmen worked. The excavations at Bedern have shown something of the physical arrangements of one medieval industry, in this case metal-working, mainly bell-founding. As we have already seen, the Bedern foundry occupied at least one long rectangular building, with a number of small square rooms to the south-west, each perhaps for a specific part of the industrial process. Throughout the foundry buildings, about a dozen hearths or furnace bases were found, for the most part constructed of pieces of roof-tile set on edge in a stiff clay, a very common surfacing technique in the Middle Ages. One of the latest, dating perhaps from the fifteenth century, was rather more complete, and showed that it was a long rectangular furnace, with probably a stokehole at either end, and tile-built side-walls. Another was built of large cobbles set in clay and formed a bowl-like firing chamber with complementary stokehole. Near it, a long shallow pit with stone and tile walls and a wooden floor may be the remains of a fuel store. The clay moulds for the bells, broken up after casting, were eventually used to surface part of the site.

The remains of a late medieval glazier's workshop were found at the City Garage, Blake Street, Thousands of fragments of glass were discovered in a pit with rubbish of about 1500. Most were plain, though some were red, blue and purple, and one was yellow. Seven plain fragments were painted, one showing part of a women's head, another part of a fleur-de-lys design. The site in Blake Street is very close to the area around the present-day St. Helen's Square where the medieval glaziers lived and worked. Further industrial evidence turned up during small-scale excavations in the aptly-named

Hornpot Lane which runs from Low Petergate to the church of Holy Trinity, Goodramgate, where a pit contained quantities of horn, the refuse of a horn-worker making cups.

External and foreign trade must also have played a major part in the economy of York, to judge from the way merchants predominated in the city's life. Neither documents nor archaeology provide as much information as we would wish. The only significant archaeological indicator of foreign trade is imported pottery. Such pieces are usually immediately recognizable to the expert, and from major medieval seaports such as Hull and Southampton are quite common. Examples are not abundant in York, however, although the city was certainly an inland port. We know that its port facilities were progressively developed throughout the Middle Ages, and striking evidence of this came from excavation of a small part of the Skeldergate river frontage. The wharf had been widened by dumping massive quantities of sand behind linked stone revetments extending into the river. This reclamation probably dates to 1305, when the King authorised the construction of a river wall, to be paid for out of local taxes intended to raise money for the city walls.

One cannot conclude even a brief archaeological survey of medieval York without looking in some detail at the Church. Its institutions—monasteries, hospitals, colleges and churches—must have been the largest and most impressive buildings in the city. Its influence permeated every aspect of life. Indeed, even in the purely secular business of the city, its role was a powerful one. It was the Church which held most of York's liberties, the areas outside the jurisdiction and control of the municipality. The city must have resounded with the clangour of church bells. There were at least 39 parish churches and numerous smaller chapels as well as the various religious houses and charitable institutions such as hospitals.

The Bedern bronze foundry. The building to the left of the alley contains a tile-built furnace.
Photo: John Bailey

Because the Church was so important, recent archaeological work has tended to concentrate on ecclesiastical institutions, including a small parish church, a medieval hospital, the College of the Vicars Choral of the Minster, and the Nunnery of St. Clement's, not to mention smaller investigations at several churches.

At the church of St. Helen-on-the-Walls, Aldwark, it was possible to carry out the complete excavation of a small parish church and a major part of its cemetery. The location of this church, demolished by the early seventeenth century, had long been in dispute. The excavation revealed its true site, and uncovered a complex building history going back certainly to the Norman period. The twelfth century church was probably a simple rectangular structure, but thirteenth century population expansion necessitated substantial rebuilding, and the nave and chancel were considerably widened, involving the demolition of all but the south and west walls of the nave. In the fourteenth century, the filling in of the great drainage ditch known as the Werkdyke allowed the church to expand still more, and a new west end was added. This seems to have been its final form. It was not possible to determine the full extent of the cemetery, but about 1100 groups of bones were eventually excavated, enough to permit a very important investigation of the medieval population of at least one small and rather poor urban parish. Of the adults buried here, men averaged 170.18 cm. and women 157.48 cm. in height, little shorter than today. At least 28 per cent of the cemetery population died before reaching adulthood. More than half the women died before reaching 35. Several cases of healed fractures may be interpreted as evidence of accidents, though three male skulls showed wounds consistent with sword-cuts. There was evidence of arthritis, gout, probable tuberculosis, rickets and other less common conditions. Study of the teeth was particularly rewarding. Of all adult jaws, 61% had lost one or more teeth, and 36% had caries. Comparisons with Roman skeletons (from Trentholme Drive) and Anglo-Scandinavians (from the Minster excavations) suggest that the later Middle Ages saw considerable changes in population-type in York.

The hospital site was that of St. Mary's in the Horsefair, off Clarence Street. In 1314, this site was relinquished by the Carmelite priory who had occupied it between 1253 and 1259, to Dean Pikering. By 1318, he had converted it into a hospital, providing a master and two assistant chaplains to support six poor and aged chaplains. It survived until the Reformation, and in 1557 was sold to the Dean and Chapter for the re-foundation of their school of St. Peter. The excavations revealed a complex development, starting in the thirteenth century when a large well-built stone structure occupied the site, probably the Carmelite priory church, which became the main structure of the hospital. The chancel would probably have been kept as the hospital chapel, with the nave re-organised for the use of the inmates, a quite normal arrangement for a medieval hospital.

At Bedern, a large part of the College of the Vicars Choral has been excavated. The Vicars Choral were men (originally 36) in minor Holy Orders who deputized for the canons of the Minster during their absences, which became increasingly frequent and prolonged during the late Middle Ages. In 1252, Archbishop Walter de Grey formally initiated the College on its site in Bedern, the first of its kind in England. From then on, the Vicars Choral became a major ecclesiastical institution in the city. The general site of the College has always been known. From the late sixteenth century onwards, however, it declined, and after the demolition of much of its property, its physical layout was lost. Only the remains of the dining hall, chapel and gatehouse are still visible. Like every medieval college, it must have had rooms or small houses for the Vicars Choral, such as can still be seen at Lincoln and Wells. We now see that there was a quadrangle of buildings around a central garden immediately to the south-west of the hall, and a separate range fronting Bedern. Clearly the hall was at one time larger than it is now. At the south-east end, a major stone building of late medieval date may have been a store-room and was clearly occupied up until modern times. A large building range was then apparently constructed at right angles to the hall, incorporating the main domestic rooms of the College, including the kitchens. Another range ran off at right angles to this one, looking out over the garden area towards the hall. A fourth substantial stone building completed the quadrangle on the north-west. A cobbled yard lay to the south-east of the domestic range. Against Bedern itself lay another range of houses. One of the buildings had a tile-built fireplace; another had well-preserved floors and apparently ran right up to and probably across Bedern, which in the Middle Ages would not have extended to meet St. Andrewgate as it does today. Within this building complex there were two brick-lined cess-pits, one of which contained a small, almost complete jug typical of the fourteenth century. A well-defined alleyway with a beaten sand surface allowed access through these buildings to Bedern from the more secluded parts of the College to the rear.

Finally, an excavation took place recently on the site of the Nunnery of St. Clement, which probably occupied the area now bounded by the Ouse and the modern streets of Clementhorpe, Vine Street and Bishopthorpe Road. At its dissolution in 1536, the sisterhood comprised a prioress and eight nuns with an annual gross income of £59. In this they ranked among the more wealthy of York's religious, though of course the York houses were all dwarfed by the Abbey of St. Mary, one of the greatest in the land, with an income in 1535 of £1650 p.a.

St. Mary's Abbey contained all the area now given over to the Yorkshire Museum and its gardens together with the King's Manor and the City Art Gallery, right up to Bootham, over 6 hectares in all. The ruins of its great church and other buildings still visible in the Museum Gardens testify to its original magnificence. St. Mary's prospered rapidly under royal patronage after 1088, and can claim to be the oldest of York's monasteries. In 1089 monks from Marmoutier (near Tours on the Loire) founded a house on the site of an apparently already ruinous church off Micklegate. The Priory of the Holy Trinity, Micklegate, thus formed was probably second only to St. Mary's in affluence and position. Its site today is almost obliterated, though the main gate survived until 1854, and part of its church survives as Holy Trinity, Micklegate.

In the early thirteenth century, a new monastic ideal arrived in England with the mendicant friars, whether inspired by the saintly Francis or the sophisticated Dominic. It was urban souls that they sought to save, and by the end of the thirteenth century, five houses were established in York alone. The Dominicans were the first, given land in 1227 near Toft Green. York's first railway station has now destroyed all trace of their priory, which housed 50 friars by 1299. They were soon followed by the Franciscans in about 1230 who moved to their permanent home between Clifford's Tower and the Ouse in 1243. By 1299 there were already 52 Franciscans and evidence suggests that they prospered exceedingly. They were joined in 1253 by the Carmelites, and finally by the Austin (Augustinian) Friars twenty years later.

Part of the site of St. Clement's Nunnery was excavated in 1976. In addition to scanty remains of buildings, several burials were uncovered. The earlier ones, all adult females, had been carefully disposed and there was evidence of shrouds and coffins. They are almost certainly the remains of the nuns and those lay persons who wished to be buried within the nunnery. These burials were in clear contrast to a later group, much less well laid out, which was probably the result of continued use of the convent cemetery after the house had been dissolved. One large grave contained over 30 burials, and was quite possibly a plague pit.

Elsewhere in the city, excavation at All Saints, Pavement, and St. Mary's Castlegate (where important, mainly pre-Conquest architectural and sculptural remains were found) and at St. Mary Bishophill Senior, have shown the importance of investigating medieval churches whenever possible, no matter how small the work that can be undertaken.

Burials in the medieval churchyard of St. Helen-on-the-Walls, Aldwark. *Photo: John Bailey*

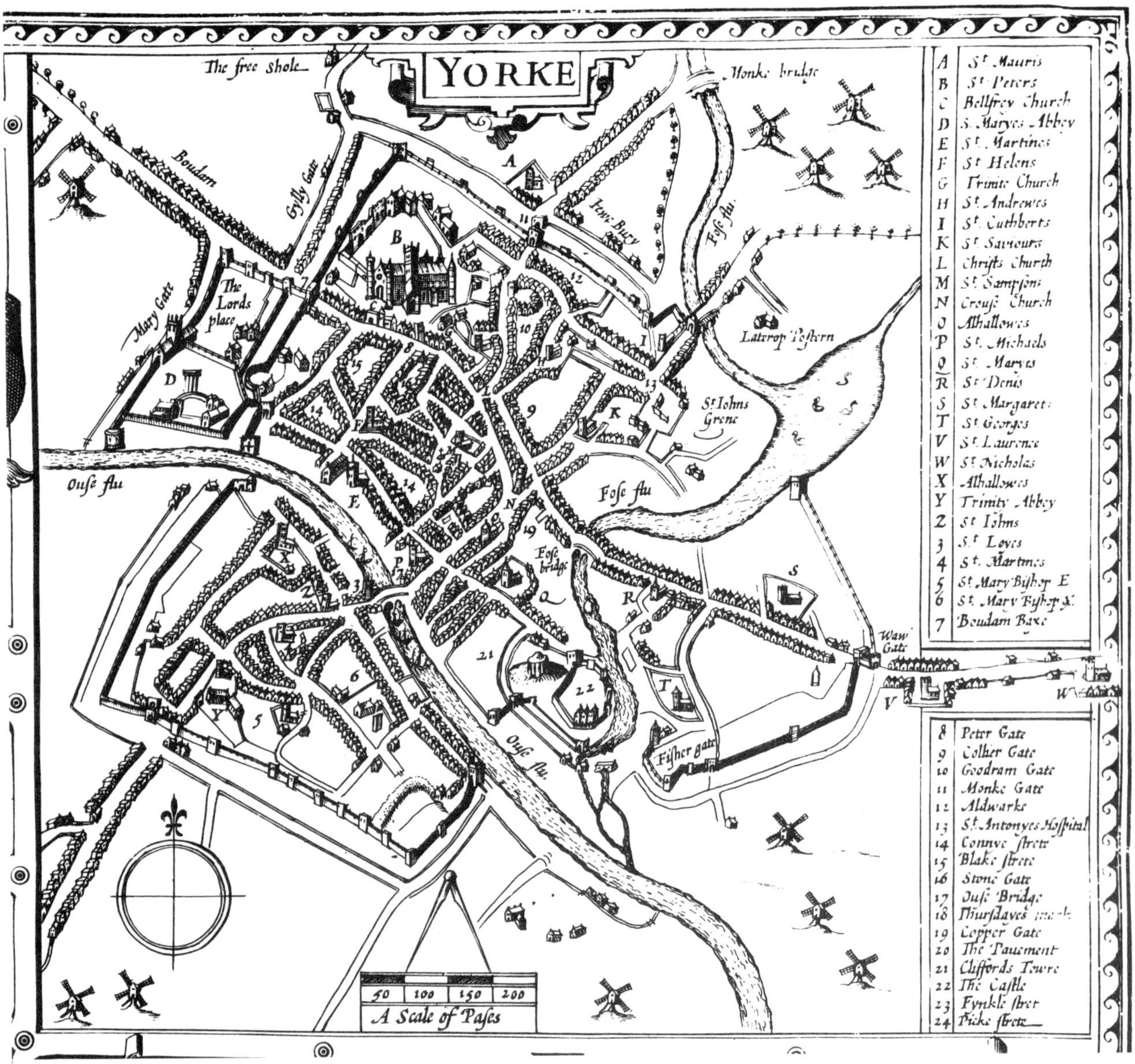

Reproduction of the map of York drawn by the eminent seventeenth century cartographer, John Speed, in 1611; an inset from his map of Yorkshire. (York Minster Library).

Post-Medieval York

In the mid-fourteenth century, York was at the height of its wealth and influence. By the second half of the fifteenth century, it was in decline. The Subsidy Rolls in 1334 show York ranking as the third highest contributor in the kingdom; by 1523, it was fifteenth. Many of the traditional trades and crafts were dying, not only because of the economic decline, but also because of technological change. The weaver was giving way to the clothier, the bowyer to the gunsmith, the stonemason and carpenter to the bricklayer. Even the great staple of wool, on which England's foreign trade had almost totally depended in the Middle Ages, collapsed towards the end of the fifteenth century and York merchants found themselves having to diversify on every side. The city as a port died as Hull eclipsed it.

Not everyone lost out in this new order, however. On the contrary, the Dissolution of the Monasteries put large new tracts of land on the market, and York Corporation was not slow to take advantage of that fact. The creation in 1526 of the powerful Council of the North, permanently resident in York at the King's Manor from 1582, did much to restore civic morale. The Council at least brought visitors to the city in need of lodging, and it is a sign of the times that innkeepers seemed to be doing well.

Municipal life was also by no means dead. In 1517 a new constitution was adopted. This did not make the city a democracy of course, but did allow for the election of a common council, and though city government remained for the most part an oligarchy of the wealthier merchants, the common council played an increasing role in local government. York's city council continued to deal as it saw fit with problems like public health and public order that it had always dealt with, and in some respects, such as laws for dealing with the poor, it acted ahead of its time.

Archaeologically, the evidence for this period is limited, primarily because the highest archaeological levels of a site are the most easily destroyed, and of course these are usually the post-medieval deposits. Nevertheless, archaeology may still demonstrate the physical development of parts of the city and the types of building within them which are often completely unrecorded in documents. Indeed this is one of the great strengths of medieval and post-medieval archaeology, and has been clearly demonstrated in the city.

At Skeldergate, for instance, the ancient division of the site between two properties was unchanged throughout the post-medieval period. There was development until the later seventeenth century when the rear of the north-west tenement progressively filled with outbuildings, first of timber on stone footings, later of brick, with latrine pits and brick drains. The back of the adjacent tenement on the other hand remained largely open, with a courtyard containing a well, and what were probably brick-built stables.

At Bedern, the foundry next to the College of the Vicars Choral ceased production at about 1500 and its buildings were given over to domestic occupation and probably used as a bakery. Although they underwent some subsequent reconstruction, their basic ground plan remained unaltered. As at Skeldergate, medieval property boundaries persisted through to modern times; indeed at the Bedern foundry the major north wall of the main building and the line of the alleyway clearly follow still extant divisions.

The College of the Vicars Choral was suppressed in 1545, only to be re-founded in 1552 on a smaller scale. In 1574 the brethren decided to abandon their ancient collegiate life, and though they continued to own property in the area until 1868, almost all the buildings were leased to tenants. Gradually the form and layout of the College disappeared under the additions and alterations occasioned by domestic occupation. Some of this later development has been investigated including several cess-pits, and large areas of garden and open yards. One such yard had a well, dug in the early sixteenth century and lined with specially made and shaped well-bricks. South of the common Hall a large square brick house, with at least three rooms on the ground floor (including a cellar) was built according to documents in about 1690. It was the best preserved post-medieval building in the excavated area, and made use of the walls of the earlier medieval domestic range, yet another example of the often amazing continuity of building lines in York. Away to the north-east, at Aldwark, a small house first built in the fourteenth century also continued in occupation, though much re-built, right up to the nineteenth century. Most of this site seems to have been given over to gardens. At the rear of the site, not far from the city walls, several long rectangular pits were excavated, filled with domestic refuse of sixteenth century date. These may be the remains of an attempt—perhaps even by the municipality—at systematic rubbish disposal. At the very least, the digger must have had a rather tidy mind!

Further down Aldwark, the church of St. Helen-on-the-Walls, already ruinous in 1575, is not shown on John Speed's map of 1610, and the site was not redeveloped, though close by to the south-east the remains of Aldwark House were revealed, brick built and dating initially to the seventeenth century. It was similar in construction to the nearby Sheldon House, which still stands.

Part of another important post-medieval house was excavated in Bishophill. Known either as Buckingham House or Duke's Hall it was owned

Union Terrace: remains of the 16th-17th century St. Peter's School, including wine cellar and latrines built over part of the medieval St. Mary's hospital. *Photo: John Bailey*

after about 1685 by the famous George Villiers, second Duke of Buckingham, and favourite of Charles II. At Buckingham's death the house fell into disrepair (it was already described in 1736 as 'daily dropping away') and all traces were finally removed in the mid-nineteenth century. There is little doubt that it was, in its day, one of the finest houses in the city. Its south-east wall was found in 1973 and is thus now established; the position of the rest of it across what is now Buckingham Street may be inferred.

Finally, the York Archaeological Trust's excavation of the medieval hospital of St. Mary in the Horsefair showed what happened from 1557 to 1644 when St. Peter's School was there. The hospital buildings were re-organized completely for the school. The west end of the hospital was demolished and a new group of buildings erected which included a kitchen block, and the probable school room. A broad ditch, pond or very large rubbish pit was dug to the west. New stone latrines and other features were built. The old chancel of the priory and hospital remained in periodic use apparently as a chapel, for burials continued to be made there. Finally, after continued re-modelling, the oldest range of buildings on the east side was demolished. School buildings continued to be extended and altered; a large brick cess-pit was made and a new oven built in the kitchen.

The archaeological study of York is a continuing one. It is a study complementary to history and for the earlier periods of the city's development is virtually the only source of evidence available. Two major points are probably worth making as a finale to this story. Archaeology by definition studies the physical remains of the past, and can thereby tell us something of the life that the documents, when they exist, may completely pass by. Secondly, experience, some of it bitter, has shown that in this study even the smallest investigation may bring unthought-of rewards. In a city like York, no hole in the ground is too small to be ignored.

Archaeological Theory

Archaeology is the study of past human societies, through the material remains of their activities. There is no aspect of human behaviour which is not of interest to the archaeologist, but his researches are normally confined to those for which tangible evidence exists. At a secondary stage, during the interpretation of his clues, he will make inferences based on common sense and a knowledge of parallel situations, so that gaps in the evidence may be filled in by informed deduction; but his primary function is to recover and record as much as possible of the physical remains of people and their activities.

There is much in common between the archaeologist and the detective. Both come on the scene of the event they wish to explain some time after the participants have disappeared. Both have developed special techniques for measuring, recording and collecting the evidence left behind. Both will make every effort to acquire not only the material evidence, but also contemporary accounts of the events (which they may or may not believe), the one by questioning witnesses and the other by searching local records. Both wish to reconstruct as faithfully as possible the true story of what happened, and will be required to write a detailed report of it, supplemented by explanatory drawings and photographs.

The chief differences between them lie in the time-scales involved and the purposes for which they carry out their investigations. Because the archaeologist comes on the scene hundreds or thousands of years after the events in which he is interested, most of his evidence will have been radically affected by the passage of time. Because the detective is in the end concerned to secure a conviction, he is satisfied once he has obtained proof of the criminal's identity and guilt. The archaeologist, however, is never satisfied that he has finished, because there is always the possibility that some aspect of the evidence may still yield information as yet unrecognized about the society he is investigating, and also because more often than not he finds himself investigating not one but several societies.

The most important, and the most obvious effect of the passage of time on the evidence found by the archaeologist, is its burial under the ground. This happens as a result of the interaction of two kinds of force, one natural and the other artificial. Under natural circumstances, an object lying on the ground will eventually become buried by the activity of small creatures such as earthworms, certain types of beetle, ants and moles that live in the upper 20-30 cm. of the earth. They create a **convectional re-distribution of the humus** around it. This process may be much accelerated by the weather, which can build up **alluvial** (silty and waterborne) or **aeolian** (windborne) **deposits** on a seasonal basis. In addition to such natural forces, wherever human beings are at work for any length of time, a much greater artifical accumulation of deposits will tend to occur, as a result of **waste-disposal** and **demolition.** Refuse will be deposited either where it is created (primary) or in reserved dumping grounds (secondary), covering any existing deposits very quickly. Demolition to make way for new buildings often creates a spread of new strata on previous surfaces, and building often entails the intentional dumping of imported material to create a suitable platform as a foundation. All these factors combine to bury archaeological evidence.

This is not to say that all archaeological evidence is to be found by digging. In specialised circumstances, such as caves or rocky, wind-swept areas, the evidence may never become buried, and is found lying just where it was left hundreds or thousands of years ago; and very old buildings that have continued to stand are themselves, as we have seen, archaeological evidence of a valuable kind. But such cases are on the whole rare, for the chances are rather small that no agency will have intervened to remove or destroy evidence that was not buried where it lay. Although burial does tend to damage some types of evidence by corrosion and decay, the fact that the débris of human activity gets buried at all is usually the main reason why it survives for the archaeologist to dig up; and it is on this fact that the chief principle of archaeology depends.

This is the **principle of stratification.** An object left lying on the ground and then buried, by natural processes of deposition will lie below a second object deposited in the same area at a later date. When found, if those processes have not been interfered with, the two objects will possess a **stratigraphic relationship** to one another, and to the surface of the ground, which is itself evidence of the different dates at which they were deposited. Although it may not at first seem obvious, not only the objects themselves, but also the tiny particles of dust, earth and other matter in which they are buried (the **context** in which they are found) were also buried in a stratigraphic order, the latest being at the top unless they have since been disturbed.

Thus, objects and soils buried at the same time will be found at roughly similar levels and the change from one level to another may be spotted by a specialist, who can record the passage of time by recording the differences between one context and another. In doing this, he relies primarily on visible changes in the colour, texture and geological constituents of the context. When he has identified these, he numbers, describes and measures them, and keep objects found in them separately from others. He is then in a position to show that Context B is earlier than Context A, and later than Context C. Such ordering of deposits is called **relative chronology,** because the age of each context and its contents is expressed in terms of its relationship to the others and not in terms of years.

Absolute chronology, which states in terms of years how long ago a deposit was laid down, may be imposed upon relative chronology in a number of different ways. In general, it depends on being able to determine a fixed point in the history of an object, and inferring that the date of its deposition must have been similar to or later than its own age, thereby placing a set of limits on the age of its context. This set of limits is often referred to as a **terminus post quem,** the **point in time after which** it must have been deposited.

Methods of establishing the exact age of an object are very numerous, and paradoxically almost all of them provide us only with estimates, stating the probability within fixed limits that the age lies between two dates. Such estimates are usually written in the following ambivalent form: e.g. 1066 ± 100. If the object to be dated is an **artifact** (one made by human agency) it may already be known in general at what period of history such objects were being made. Classified lists of particular kinds of artifacts, especially pottery, are drawn up by archaeologists in chronological order, and are referred to as **typologies.** They permit a date-bracket to be identified for the artifact, and thereby a range of possible **termini post quos** for its context. If there is information written on the artifact (as for example there often is on coins, tombstones, military equipment or on tobacco-pipes) the date-bracket may be narrowed down to perhaps quite small limits. But the unknown factor almost always exists; how long a time elapsed between the date of manufacture and the date of deposition?

If the object is **organic** (made of once-living material) such as wood, bone, flax, etc., it may be possible to submit it to laboratory tests which will show when it stopped living. This is done by measuring the amount of **radiocarbon** (carbon isotope 14) it contains, for all living things absorb C_{14} during their lifetime, and begin to lose it at a steady rate when they die. So the bones of a skeleton can be tested to see when the subject died, the charcoal from a fire can be tested to see when the firewood was chopped from the tree, or the threads from a cloth may be tested to see when the flax was harvested or the wool sheared from the sheep. But none of these dates is necessarily, or even probably, that at which the object was deposited, though they are all of necessity **termini post quos.**

If the object is **inorganic** and known to have been heated in antiquity, such as pottery or brick (but excluding metals), the energy it has accumulated since then may be released in the form of **thermoluminescence,** which may be measured and related to the number of years which have elapsed since it was last heated above 100°C. This may be the time when it was fired in the kiln, or of course it may just be the time when it was last caught in a fire of any description. So this method is rather problematical to use.

There are other methods (**potassium argon dating, fission-track dating, archaeomagnetic dating**) and no doubt fresh ones will be developed as research progresses. The process of **dendrochronological dating,** for example, which identifies sequences of tree-ring growth with dated sequences of seasonal rainfall, has advanced to the point where it can be used to correct anomalies in radiocarbon dating results. But they all fail, more or less seriously, to date the context in which the object was found, except by inference. The deposits themselves, however, may be examined for other types of evidence. They may contain microscopic organic remains; in York, they frequently do. If **pollens,** for example, or **seeds** are preserved, analysis may show what kinds of vegetation existed nearby the deposits as they were laid down. The analyst may known from parallel cases that the species involved last grew in that area at a given period. At any rate he will be able to suggest how, if at all, the local vegetation has changed, and perhaps what crops were being planted. Similarly, **microfaunal remains** (parasites, insects, beetles, etc.) may enable the specialist to suggest what conditions prevailed to permit colonisation by these organisms, and how they differed from those of today.

In the end, however, the interpretation will depend, from a chronological point of view, on the stratigraphy. If Phase B is above Phase C, and below Phase A, then the **terminus post quem** of Phase A is, at the very least, the **terminus ante quem** (the **point in time before which**) Phase B must have been deposited. The lower limit of Phase B will similarly fix the upper limit of Phase C. The process of archaeological dating is for the most part a constant matter of narrowing down such possibilities.

Contrary to popular belief, however, dating the remains is not the only or even the most important function of the archaeologist. Much more desirable than knowing when these objects came here, is knowing why they came here, what their purpose was, and who caused them to be where they are. If the answers to these questions are known, the date will usually be self-evident. Whole books have been written, and remain to be written, on the ways in which these problems may be dealt with. In general, the archaeologist must recognize the remains of features for what they are or might be, disentangle their stratigraphic relationship to one another, and seek in the proper quarters the specialised knowledge which may elucidate them further. Thus for example he must know a grave-shaft when he sees one, and trace its exact dimensions and the point from which it was dug. He may then need an anatomical specialist to tell him the age, sex and pathology of the skeleton, a ceramics expert to identify the date and origin of the pottery found with it, and a numismatist to pronounce on the coins in its mouth. Having collected all this information, and added some of his own about the type of funerary practice represented, he may then draw it all together and offer an interpretation which perhaps not one of the individual specialists could have made alone.

In the end, however, it is a matter of combining common sense with detailed examination, both of the new evidence, and of past interpretations of similar evidence. The archaeologist cannot afford not to familiarise himself with previously recorded examples of what he has found, and this may mean long hours in the library. If a little is known, a little more may be added by careful comparison. Whole generations of archaeologists may live, work and die before the true meaning of everything they dig up is realised.

This does not prevent them from meticulously recording what they do find, whether they understand it or not. Every object and complex association of objects must be examined for the light it may throw on the economy of the people, their technological level, the diseases they were prone to, their political and religious behaviour, and any other aspect whatever of their society which may be illuminated by such study. Each case is unique, and each is the last chance we have to examine it. For the most important thing to remember about the excavation of archaeological material is that it not only recovers the evidence, but also destroys it. The situation an archaeologist finds when he excavates a site is unique. It has been building up century by century until he lays it bare.

In so doing, he is recording it for posterity; but he is also removing it altogether. He therefore carries a grave responsibility to record accurately, objectively and as comprehensively as possible, for it can never be done again. In addition, he has an equal responsibility to make his information available to other people both now and in the future, for it is of no benefit if it cannot be used, and he has eliminated the possibility of anyone else repeating the work. It is clear, therefore, that archaeological evidence should never be disturbed except by qualified archaeologists who have the means to carry through what they have begun. The only exceptions to this rule are sites which are already being destroyed by some other agency, and even then every effort should be made to use professional techniques in rescuing the evidence. The result otherwise will be the permanent loss of another unique fragment of our history, too much of which has already disappeared.

Further Reading

The following publications, arranged in order of their relevance to successive subjects treated in this booklet, will be of interest to those who wish to follow up the archaeology and history of York in more detail:

Royal Commission on Historical Monuments. *City of York, I: Eboracum.* (H.M.S.O. 1962)

Butler, R. M. (Ed.). *Soldier and Civilian in Roman Yorkshire.* (Leicester University Press. 1971)

Cramp, R. *Anglian and Viking York.* (Borthwick Papers, No. 33. York. 1967)

Hall, R. A. *The Viking Kingdom of York.* (Yorkshire Museum and Y.A.T. 1976)

Hall, R. A. (Ed.). *Viking-Age York and the North.* (Council for British Archaeology. 1978)

Raine, A. *Medieval York.* (John Murray. London. 1955)

Royal Commission on Historical Monuments. *City of York, II: The Defences.* (H.M.S.O. 1972)

Stacpoole, A. (Ed.). *The Noble City of York.* (Cerealis Press. York. 1972)

Wilson, David. *Science and Archaeology.* (Penguin. 1978)

The results of recent excavations by York Archaeological Trust are summarised in the Trust's quarterly bulletin, *Interim*, which also contains articles giving background information, and is available by subscription from INTERIM, York Archaeological Trust, 47 Aldwark, York YO1 2BX. Overseas subscribers should use International Money Order or add Bank Clearance charge to their cheques.

Final Reports on the Trust's work appear in the fascicule series *The Archaeology of York*, Ed. P. V. Addyman, published by the Council for British Archaeology. The following titles are available:

AY 3/1 *The Church Street Sewer and an Adjacent Building.* J. B. Whitwell

AY 3/2 *Interval Tower SW5 and the South-West Defences: Excavations 1972-75.* A. B. Sumpter and S. Coll

AY 4/1 *Riverside Structures and a Well in Skeldergate and Buildings in Bishophill.* M. O. H. Carver, S. Donaghey and A. B. Sumpter

AY 14/1 *The Environmental Evidence from the Church Street Roman Sewer.* P. C. Buckland

AY 17/1 *Finds from a Roman Sewer System and an Adjacent Building in Church Street.* Arthur MacGregor

AY 17/2 *Roman Finds from Bishophill and Skeldergate.* Arthur MacGregor

AY 19/1 *The Analysis of Archaeological Insect Assemblages: A New Approach.* Harry K. Kenward